Creative DIY
Watercolor Christmas

Easy and Enjoyable Projects Coloring Your Own Holidays

Contents

Introduction

Unleash Your Inner Artist and Create a Festive Masterpiece!

Are you ready to add a touch of holiday cheer to your home? With Creative DIY Watercolor Christmas, you can turn your artistic vision into a beautiful Christmas creation. This step-by-step guide will lead you through the process of painting your very own Christmas scene, from the twinkling lights on a snowy tree to the cozy fireplace in a winter wonderland.

Whether you're a seasoned painter or just starting out, this book is designed to make your holiday crafting experience enjoyable and rewarding. With clear instructions, helpful tips, illustrations, you'll have everything you need to bring your Christmas dreams to life on canvas. So grab your brushes, choose your colors, and let your imagination run

Materials and Equipment

Watercolor Paint

Watercolor paints are made from finely ground pigments held together with a water-soluble binder that fixes the pigment onto the paper. They come in solid, moist and liquid forms; you can use them by themselves or mix and match them together.

Brushes

There is a huge selection of brushes available, and you can choose from ones made from synthetic, mixed fiber or natural hair. You will need variety of brushes shape to achieve specific shapes -circle, lines, leaves,... Many artist prefer natural hair because they can hold a lot of water, but personally I like to use synthetic brushes as they are easier to take care of and can last for years.

Palette

For mixing watercolor tube paints and inks. Porcelain ones are the best: the paint stays moist longer, the pigments are easier to mix and they don't stain, making them very easy to clean. If you don't have a porcelain palette, a porcelain works just as well.

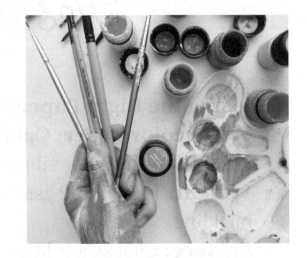

Jars of Water

Line these up to wash your brushes and avoid contaminating your palette when using different colors.

Pencil and Eraser

You may choose to sketch and draw an outline so keep a pencil handy. Use the eraser to erase any visible lines at the end.

Tips and Tricks

Choosing the Right Paper:
- **Watercolor Paper:** Opt for 100% cotton paper for better absorption and color vibrancy.
- **Weight:** 140 lb (300 gsm) or heavier is ideal for preventing buckling.
- **Surface:** Choose a cold-pressed surface for a slightly textured effect, or a hot-pressed surface for a smoother finish.

Christmas-Inspired Watercolor Ideas:
- **Ornaments:** Paint circular shapes and add details like bows, snowflakes, or stars.
- **Wreaths:** Create circular wreaths with green and red washes, and add pine needles, berries, or bows.
- **Gift Tags:** Paint small tags with holiday messages and festive designs.
- **Cards:** Design unique Christmas cards with personalized messages and illustrations.
- **Gift Wrapping Paper:** Paint patterns or designs on plain wrapping paper.

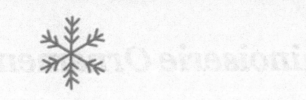

Christmas
Projects

Chinoiserie Ornaments

SUPPLIES:
- White glass ornaments
- Artist brush #3
- Blue sharpie paint (ulta fine) & (fine tip)
- Alcohol

Step 1: With a cotton ball clean all the ornaments with alcohol. With an ultra-fine tip sharpie on paper and start drawing the flower petal. Make 5 petal drops where they both meet at the end. Here are some sample petals

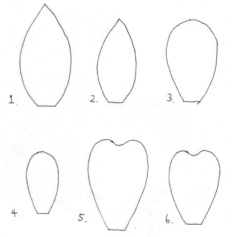

Step 2: With the extra fine sharpie draw a long line connecting all the flowers.

Step 3: With a #3 artist paintbrush paint the inside of the flower carefully

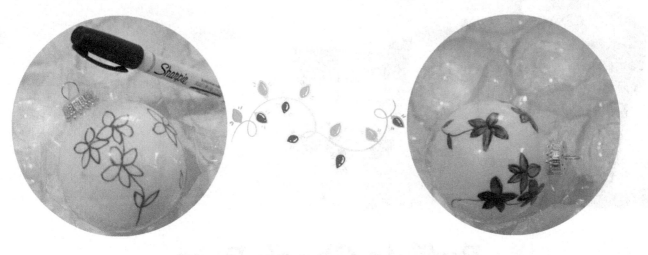

Step 4: Draw little leaves on the long stems. Here is a small diagram you can practice on paper.

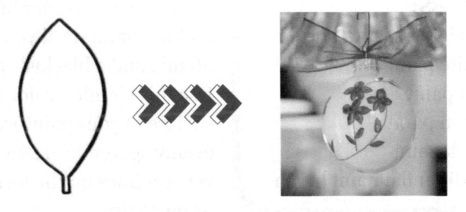

Buffalo Check Pots

SUPPLIES:
- Small terra cotta pots
- White paint
- Red paint
- Green paint
- Black paint
- Medium flat paint brush

Step 1: On a mixing tray or paper plate, blend together black paint and red paint until you have a 50-50 mix and a blackish-red color. Use this blended color and the flat surface of your paintbrush to paint evenly spaced horizontal and vertical lines on the terra-cotta pot. Allow to dry.

9

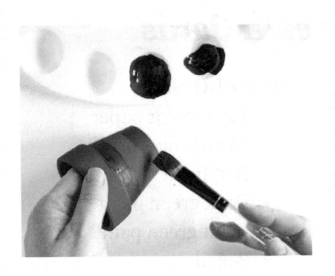

Step 2: Use black paint to fill in the squares where your lines overlap. Let your pots dry.

Step 3: Repeat the above steps to make white and the green pots, using the white and green paint to mix with your black paint.

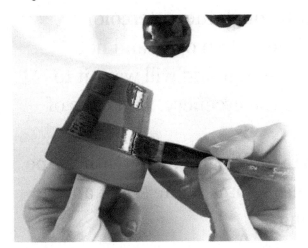

Christmas Wreath Cards

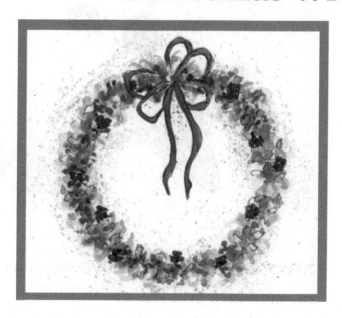

SUPPLIES:
- Watercolor paper
- Watercolor brush
- Red paint
- Dark green paint
- Light green paint
- Pencil
- Black pen
- Kneaded eraser

Step 1: Lightly trace around a round object in pencil. Draw a bow. Keep the pencil light so it doesn't show through the watercolor.

Step 2: Paint the bow leaving some of the ribbon open and not connected. You will be filling in green around it and will want it to look like the ribbon is hidden by some of the greenery. Add dabs of red paint to look like clusters of berries.

Step 3: Use a yellow green paint and start filling in the wreath shape with dabs and small strokes of paint. Leave some white space and keep the edges loose and random looking.

Step 4: Add a medium green color to the wreath using small, loose strokes. Don't cover up all of the yellow green-these are your highlights. Add some dark green in places on top of the medium green. Use a variety of greens and dark blues. Keep the edges loose and open. Add some darker color here and there to the ribbon and berries.

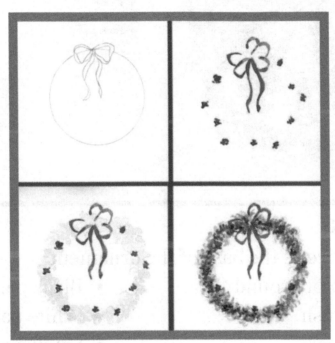

Step 5: I added a little bit of pen detail on the bow and a few berry and leaf shapes. I used a very, very fine point black pen and tried not to make it too dark or overpowering.

Starrynight Wood Ornaments

SUPPLIES:

- Wood slice as the base of the ornament
- Watercolor ground
- Paint brush
- Sandpaper
- Paint palette
- Metallic purple paint
- Metallic blue paint
- Black paint
- White paint
- Small eye hook
- Gloss varnish
- Brush round #2
- Brush round #10

Step 1: Choose a round slice of wood for your ornament and clean any debris off the front side. Using a firm brush, such as an acrylic brush, paint a thin coat of watercolor ground on the wood. If the watercolor ground is too thick mix water into the ground on a palette. Paint three thin coats of watercolor ground on the wood slice allowing it to dry between each coat.

Step 2: Once the watercolor ground is dry sand any rough places left from the painting the ground. Sand very lightly trying not to sand the ground down to the wood.

Step 3: Begin with purple at the top and fade it out halfway down. Then paint the blue starting at the bottom, also fading to the middle where the two colors blend. Once the two colors are blended smoothly, let the paint dry before adding a second coat.

Step 4: With a small paintbrush, such as brush round #2, use black to paint lines for the tree trunks. Angle the lines toward the center of the wood making each a different height. Paint the branches on each tree starting at the top where it is narrow making the tree wider at the bottom. Let it dry.

Step 5: Paint just a few darker lines down the left side of each tree. Then using a small amount of white paint, add a few lines of white down the right side of each tree. By placing the dark black on one side next to the lighter white on the other the trees appear three - layers.

Step 6: With the brush round #2 brush white paint add dots of white to the sky for stars. An opened paperclip is also a great option to dip in the paint for more control when adding stars.

Step 7: Add a light coat of spray gloss varnish to the painting. This will help keep the painting on the ornament from fading, protect it from liquid, and add a little extra shine. Remember do not spray inside, I always take it to the back porch for this step. Let the varnish dry completely.

Step 8: Carefully choose the spot to place the small eye hook at the top of the ornament. Screw the hook directly into the top side of the ornament. Once the hook is secure add twine and tie it together so the ornament is ready to hang. Add a signature and date to the back and you have a one-of-a-kind keepsake to enjoy or share.

Christmas Lights Painting

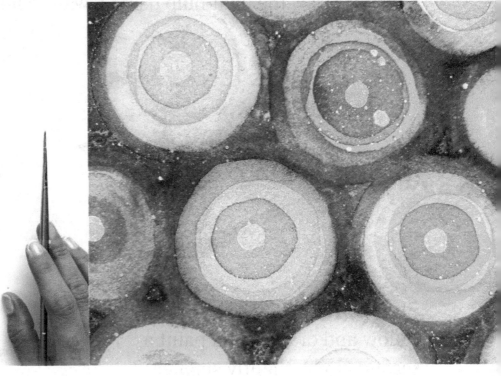

SUPPLIES:

- Paint palette
- Pencil or watercolor pencil
- White paint
- Dark blue paint
- Light blue paint
- Green paint
- Orange paint
- Medium flat paint brush
- Watercolor paper

Step 1: Paint a translucid yellow circle and let dry.
Step 2: Draw the light bulb using a watercolor pencil.

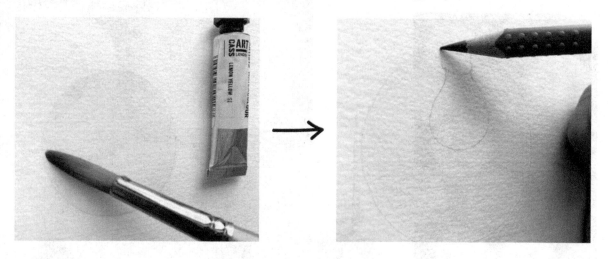

Step 3: Make a watery mix of yellow and orange, and paint a second circle, slightly smaller than the first. Go around the light bulb in step 3 and 4, we want to reserve the original color. Allow to dry.
Step 4: Add more orange to your mix and paint a third smaller circle.

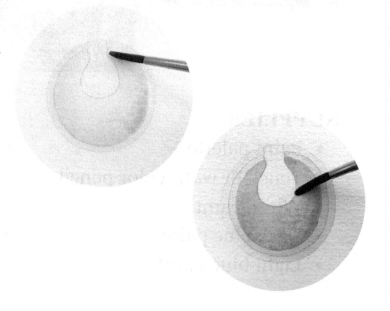

Step 5: Repeat this step if you wish with smaller circles, I painted a total of five circles.

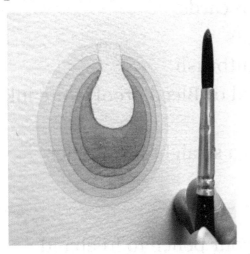

Step 6: Leave the light bulb as is or add more color if you wish. Using a gray watercolor pencil, draw the base of the light bulb.

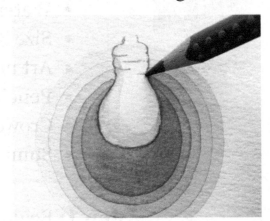

Step 7: Try it using different colors!

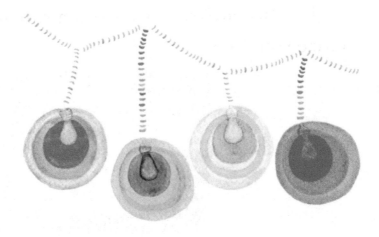

Blown Ornaments Cards

SUPPLIES:
- Blank watercolor cards
- Watercolor paints
- Size 3 (-ish) paintbrush
- Art masking fluid or Bleed proof white ink
- Pencil
- Crowquill nib in a straight pen holder
- Sumi ink

Step 1: Begin by using your pencil to freehand draw 5-6 different sizes of circles on your watercolor card. Vary the size and positioning of each of the circles. Next, draw a cap on top of each circle you drew.

Step 2: Now, draw a small semicircle on top of each cap. Once you've drawn the ornaments, draw a banner in the upper left part of the card. Use the calligraphy style of your choice to write "happy holidays" in the banner.

Step 3: Finish up by using a ruler or a straight edge to draw vertical lines that extend from the top center of the semicircles to the top of the card.

Step 4: This step is optional, depending on whether you have art masking fluid. If you don't have, you can use bleed proof white ink. If you do, use a small (size 1-ish) paint brush to apply two contoured lines to the right side of each ornament.

Step 5: Give your masking fluid a minute or two to dry, then use a medium paintbrush (size 3-ish) to paint over your first circle with watercolor. Be sure to paint a little bit outside the lines, and make it a point to get some paint on the cap as well! urn the card upside down, and blow on the watercolor paint until it streaks out the bottom and/or sides of the circle.

Step 6: If you opted to draw a banner, go ahead and paint that in with a nice, neutral color. For the banner, you will paint in the lines.

Step 7: Give your paint a few minutes to completely dry, then trace over all of your pencil guidelines with black ink such as sumi. To make a bow, you'll first draw two slightly shaky ovals on either side of the vertical line that intersects the semicircle. Each oval should come to a point at the intersection of the vertical line and the semicircle. Next, draw two wavy, short lines coming from the bottom of the vertical line/semicircle intersection.

Step 8: The only thing left to do is add your highlights. You can do this one of two ways. If you used masking fluid, rub an eraser over it; it will come right off. If you didn't use masking fluid for this project, you'll use a small paintbrush and bleed proof white ink to paint highlights directly onto the ornaments.

Santa Stones

SUPPLIES:

- Smooth beach stones
- Gesso or a similar primer (this will give you better coverage)
- Red paint
- Paint brushes
- Skin tone paint
- White paint
- Black paint
- Satin craft varnish (protects paint and adds vibrance/sheen)

Step 1: Scrub stones to remove any grit and debris and let them dry. Your stones will dry quickly in a warm, sunny spot, but you can speed up the drying process with a hairdryer.

Step 2: Paint the stones with a coat of Gesso or a similar craft primer. If you don't have primer, that's ok, but you may need several coats of paint to get full coverage.

Step 3: You can leave the back of your Santa stones unpainted, or you can paint them in a solid colour or with a second Santa face. Give each band of colour a second coat of paint and allow to dry.

Step 4: Dip the handle of a paintbrush into some paint to dot on Santa's pom pom, eyes and nose.

Step 5: Once your Santa stones are completely dry, brush them with a coat of satin craft varnish to protect your paint and to intensify your colours and add sheen.

Wreath Wood Ornaments

SUPPLIES:

- Green paint
- Yellow paint
- Blue paint
- White paint
- Red paint
- Jute string
- Water for rinsing your brush
- Two paint brushes (a small round watercolor and a small flat paintbrush)
- Wood slice or wood round
- Drill (optional)

Step 1: Paint the background of your wood slice with white paint using your small flat brush. Let dry.

Step 2: Mix the yellow and blue acrylic paint to mix a light green color. Use the small round brush to draw a circle on your wood slice.

Step 3: Make your way around the circle and paint simple leaves going in the same direction

Step 4: Use your darker green paint to paint some evergreens in your wreath by drawing a line with simple lines coming out of each side. Repeat these around the entire circle.

Step 5: Paint the berries by using your red paint and making small circles placed around the wreath.

Step 6: Using a drill, create a small hole in the top of the ornament. You can also buy pre-drilled wood slices if you don't have a drill.

Snowman Spoons

SUPPLIES:

- Wooden spoon/spatula
- White paint
- Black paint
- Light blue paint
- Chenille stems
- Pom poms
- Wiggle eyes
- Wooden snowflake sticker
- Rhinestone
- Paintbrush
- Glue gun and glue sticks
- Ribbons
- Buttons
- Ruler
- Scissors
- Craft stick
- Craft foam

Step 1: Gather all supplies. Basecoat the wooden spoons and spatula with white acrylic craft paint. Let dry and apply a second coat, if necessary.

Step 2: Using scissors, cut the rounded ends off a wooden craft stick. Paint the craft stick and top 1/3 of wooden spatula with black acrylic craft paint. Let dry and apply a second coat, if necessary.

Step 3: To create carrot noses, cut three triangles from orange craft foam. Attach two wiggle eyes and a carrot nose to each wooden spoon for the snowman face. To create the earmuffs, measure and cut a chenille stem to 4" long. Bend into a "U" shape and glue to either side of the wooden spoon. Attach pom poms over the cut end of each stem using a glue gun and glue sticks. Glue the black craft stick to the wooden spatula to create the hat brim.

Step 4: Create the snowmen mouths by dipping the end of a paintbrush handle into black acrylic craft paint. It makes perfectly round dots!

Step 5: Tie ribbon scarves around the neck of each snowman, securing with a dot of glue. Attach two black buttons to the handle of each wooden spoon with a glue gun and glue sticks.

Step 6: Basecoat a wooden snowflake sticker with light blue acrylic craft paint. Attach to the wooden spatula snowman hat with a glue gun and glue sticks. To finish, place a self-adhesive rhinestone in the center of the snowflake.

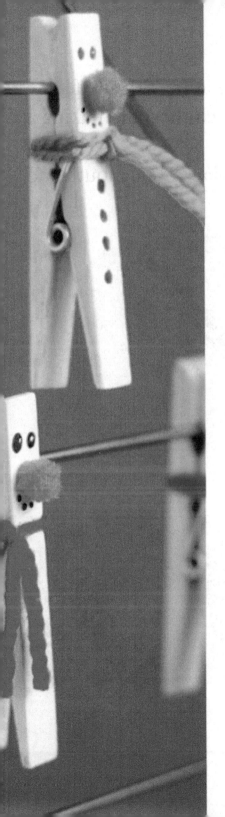

Snowman Clothspins

SUPPLIES:

- Natural wood clothespins
- Yarn in various colors
- Glue
- Orange mini pom poms
- White paint
- Paint brush
- Black marker
- Scissors

Step 1: Start by paining the clothespins with white paint. Depending on the wood and paint you might need to do more than one layers. Be careful as the paint can "glue" the clothespin, open it up a few times while it dries.

Step 2: Once the paint dries completely, it's time to make a scarf. Take a short piece of yarn and wrap it around the clothespin, making a know. Add a drop of glue to secure it.

Step 3: Now take a black marker and draw two black eyes, mouth and black buttons on the snowman body.

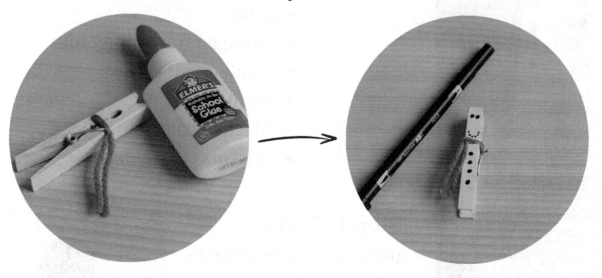

Step 4: Add a drop of glue between the eyes and mouth and stick on an orange mini pom pom. Wait for the glue to dry and your clothespin snowman craft is done.

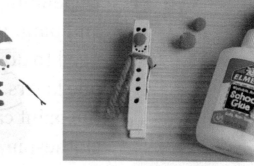

Ice Cream Ornamanets

SUPPLIES:
- Mini terra cotta pots
- Mini ornaments balls
- Watercolor paint
- Paint brushes
- Hot glue gun
- Cherry embellishment

Step 1: Start by painting your ornaments with watercolor paint.
NOTE: I did two coats of paint so that there would be no streaks and the ornament would have full coverage.

Step 2: While the ornament is drying, paint the top of the mini flower pot the same ice cream color and add some cute ice cream drips.

Step 3: Add a cone pattern to the flower pot with a brown paint pen.

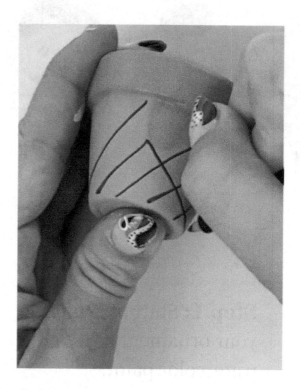

Step 4: Once the paint is completely dry you can also add white highlights to the ice cream drips to help them stand out.

Step 5: On the ornament, paint any topping you'd like (whipped cream, chocolate sauce, caramel, etc).

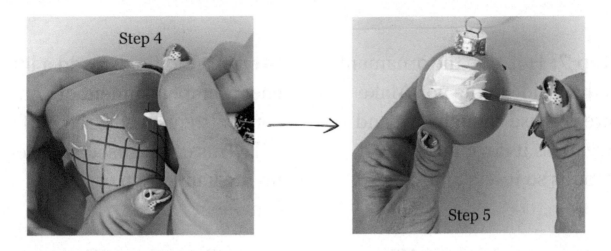

Step 6: While you topping paint is drying, add the face using paint pens. Next, add sprinkles or whatever ever fun design you'd like to the top of the ornament.

NOTE: Make sure the paint is completely dry before adding details with the paint pens.

Step 7: Hot glue the ornament to the inside of the pot. Make sure you use enough glue and give press it down for a few seconds so it sets and sticks!

Step 8: And finally, add a little cherry embellishment or you could also just use a red puff ball. This can be used to cover up the hanger top of the ornament.

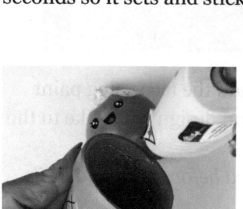

Gingerbread Mini Pots

SUPPLIES:

- Mini flower pots
- Wooden beads (1 big and 2 small)
- Brown paint
- White paint
- Rose paint
- Paintbrush
- Black marker
- 2 buttons
- Silk ribbon
- Pencil
- Hot glue

Step 1: Paint the pot and the wooden beads brown. Paint a wavy line with white paint on them.

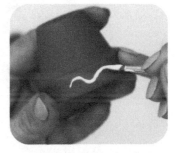

Step 2: Draw the face of the gingerbread on the biggest wooden beads. Glue that on the top of the pot.

Step 3: Glue the two smaller wooden beads to the right and left side.
Step 4: Glue the buttons on the pot.
Step 5: Make a bow with the silk ribbon and glue it up under the head.

Snowmen Paintings

SUPPLIES:
- Scissors
- Paint brush(s)
- Pink paint
- Pre-made yarn pom-poms
- Mini canvas
- Black paint
- Orange paint
- Glue gun

Step 1: Using paint brushes and paint, paint your snowman's face to your preference on your mini canvas (refer to imagery above and below.) Allow adequate time for drying.

Step 2: Snip about 1" off of the pipe cleaner. Using low-temp hot glue, affix the pipe cleaner in an upside down U shape onto either (top) side of the mini canvas. Hold in place until hot glue sets. Add a large yarn pom-pom to either side, also using low-temp hot glue, to create the look of earmuffs. Hold in each pom-pom in place until hot glue sets. The pipe cleaner portion of the earmuffs also doubles as a hanger for your mini canvas snowman ornament.

Step 3: Hang your completed mini canvas snowman ornament and enjoy or gift to someone special this holiday season!

Christmas Tree Napkins

SUPPLIES:

- Cocktail napkins
- Paint brushes
- Sewing machine
- Darning foot
- Red paint
- Green paint
- Yellow-green paint
- Black or brown paint
- Washable fabric marker or a light pencil
- Thin permanent marker (if you don't have a sewing machine)

Step 1: Once you have picked your design (and feel free to use this one), draw a very light outline with a washable fabric marker or light pencil.

Step 2: Once you have drawn your design, apply the paint. Do not paint the area where you intend to paint another color, such as red paint. Just leave those areas blank.

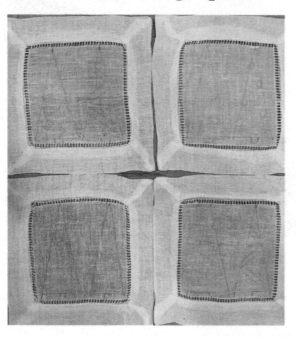 

Step 3: Paint the entire trees, including the yellow stars on top. Let dry. All you need to do is iron the napkin to set the acrylic paint and you are done.

Step 4: Place the darning foot on your sewing machine and stitch the outline of the design. Stitch everywhere twice.

Step 5: If you don't like to sew, you can use a permanent thin marker and achieve the same look without a sewing machine.

Step 6: Stitch the second tree and you're done!

Step 3

Step 4

Step 5

Step 6

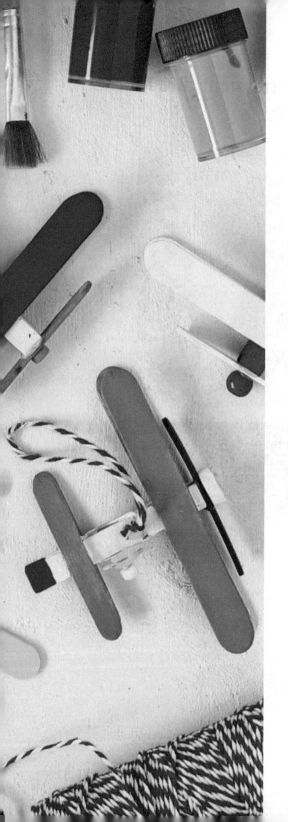

Popsicle Stick Airplane

SUPPLIES:
- Wide popsicle sticks
- Small popsicle sticks
- Wooden clothespins
- Wood bead or button or bobble
- Hot glue
- Watercorlor paint
- Baker's Twine

Step 1: Paint the craft sticks and let them dry completely. If you don't want the mess of paint, here are three options you can try instead:

- Buy pre-colored craft sticks and pre-colored clothespins.
- Use washable marker to color right on the wood.
- Cover the wood with washi tape like I did with these popsicle stick sled ornaments

Step 2: Assemble the airplane as show in these pictures:

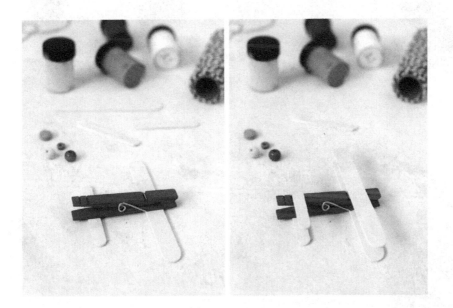

Attach the craft stick wings to the bottom side of the clothespin, then another set of wings on the top side of the clothespin. The craft glue pens work great for kids to help them apply the glue precisely. They are easy for small hands to control.

Step 3: Add the last small craft stick to the front of the clothespin (it's the propeller) and glue the wood bead into place right in the center. This part really does need to be done with hot glue or else it falls off too easily.

Step 4: Hot glue a loop of baker's twine to the clothespin right behind the front wing. The loop will be used to hang the ornament from the Christmas tree.

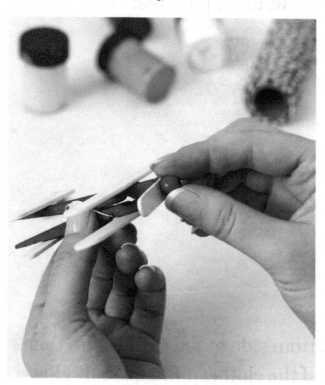

Christmas Row House

SUPPLIES:

- Rustic bird house wood panel
- Craft Paint
- Cardstock and vellum
- Watercolor paint
- Fine tip glue pen
- Assorted miniatures: wreaths, trees...
- Fairy lights
- Glitter snow
- Mod poge

Step 1: Paint the wood. I chose vintage pastel colors just for fun, but you could definitely go more traditional with red and green. Paint the roofs white so they look like they're covered in snow.

Step 2: Make all of the windows and doors. If you don't have a craft cutting machine, you can definitely cut these by hand, it would just take longer. I lined all of the windows with vellum to mimic the look of glass. It worked surprisingly well! I recommend using a fine-tip glue pen to glue all of these small pieces together. I lined the back of each door with a piece of craft foam to make them stick up off of the houses and add dimension.

Step 3: Add details. I added miniature wreaths and trees, a little snowman made of pom poms and a mini picket fence. To make the garland on the fence, I cut up two of the mini wreaths. The knobs on the doors are little golden beads. Don't skimp on the details... that's what makes this project fun!

Step 4: Brush mod podge anywhere you want snow to pile (along the bottom of the houses, on windowsills, on the roof, etc.) then sprinkle the fake snow onto the wet Mod Podge to make it stick. It's best to work in small sections so the glue doesn't dry before you can sprinkle it with snow.

Step 5: Add lights! I used hot glue to secure little LED star shaped lights all along the rooftop. Then I glued fake mini Christmas bulbs on top just for fun. Glue the battery pack to the back of the sign, making sure you can still access the batteries and on/off switch.

Vintage Ornaments Pillows

SUPPLIES:

- One pillow cover, 18" x 18" or 20" x 20"
- Paint brushes
- One spoon in Black
- Sewing nachine
- Washable Fabric Marker
- Red paint
- Green paint
- Gray pant
- Darning foot

Step 1: Find a design and cut out templates to use for tracing.

Step 2: Place the ornaments on the pillow in a design that you like. Trace the ornaments with the washable fabric marker.

Step 3: One you are done tracing the ornaments, add the hanging lines with a long ruler.

  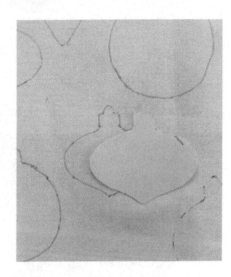

Step 4: Mix the paint. I like to keep it simple so I primarily used just red and green.

Step 5: Open up the pillow and place a piece of cardboard or parchmnet inside. this will prevent any paint from soaking through to the backside of the pillow. Paint each ornament. I added a warm highlight on the right side of each one. Let the pillow dry.

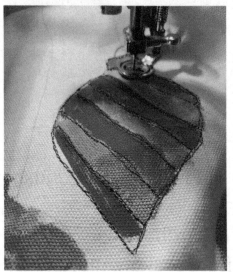

Step 6: Add the stitch embroidery. Be careful not to sew on the underneath side of the pillow. Begin stitching a very loose ornament pattern on top of each ornament. It doesn't have to be exact, just stitch two rounds of stitching on each ornament. Since I used an already made pillow cover, I opened it up and stitched each ornament carefully, being sure not to stitch the underside of the pillow cover. It's not hard, I promise! You can see in the photo what the sewing machine pressure foot looks like. The difference from regular sewing is that you get to move the fabric which is awesome. Since you control where the fabric moves you can stitch in any direction you want! The good thing is that the stitching does not have to be perfect. I like it better if it's not perfect.

Christmas Tree Bottle Stoppers

SUPPLIES:

- Unfinished wood christmas trees
- Cork bottle stoppers
- Watercolor paints
- Paint brushes
- E6000 glue (or any kind of strong glue)
- Clear satin spray paint

Step 1: Start by giving the blank wood trees an even coat of paint in whatever base color you would like. I mixed up a variety of shades of green using a few different green acrylic paints I had in my craft stash. Then I painted the bottom trunk of the trees with a tan/brown Fawn color. I used about 2-3 coats of each color of paint to completely cover the wood surface.

Step 2: Now comes the creative part — decorating your little trees! Use a thin paint brush or paint markers to draw on all the tiny details to bring your Christmas trees to life. There are so many different patterns you can do, polka dots for ornaments, string lights by adding lines of dots, scalloped edges,.... And the best part is if you mess up or you don't like your original design, you can just repaint the whole tree again and start over

Step 3: Once you're happy with your Christmas tree designs, and you have allowed the paint to fully dry, it is time to seal and protect your work. Take the trees outside and give them a few even coats of a satin clear spray paint. This will help seal and protect the surface for continuous use.

Step 4: Once the clear coat has fully dried, you can glue your Christmas trees to your cork bottle stoppers. To do this, place your corks upright on your table with the narrow side down. Now squeeze a tiny dab of E6000 glue (or any kind of permanent adhesive) to the bottom of each Christmas tree trunk. Then gently press the trees onto the center of each cork and leave the glue to dry overnight. Because E6000 glue takes a little while to set, it is best to leave the trees standing in the upright position overnight while the glue dries.

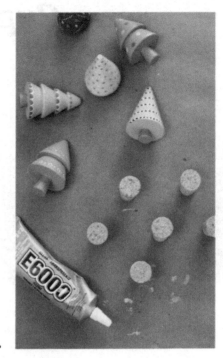

Cupcake Ornaments

SUPPLIES:

- Clear plastic ornaments
- Fine glitter
- Watercolor paint
- Watercolor paint markers
- Cupcake liner
- Polycrylic clear gloss
- Medicine dropper/syringe
- Hot glue gun

Step 1: Start by creating your glitter ornaments. Fill a medicine dropper with about 5ml of polycrylic. Squeeze the polycrylic from the dropper into the ornament.

Step 2: Swirl the liquid around the entire ornament until it is completely coated. Turn over the ornament and let the excess liquid drain. I used tiny cups to allow the liquid to drain so that I could coat 2-3 ornaments at a time. You can always pour the excess liquid back into the polycrylic can.

Step 3: Pour glitter directly into the ornament. I didn't need a funnel because the glitter opening poured easily, but you can use a funnel if needed.

Step 4: Swirl the ornament to cover the inside with glitter. To get the last little bit of the top covered take a piece of paper and place it over the top and give the ornament a few shakes.

Step 5: You don't have to but it's a good idea to let the ornament dry for 15-20 mins if possible.

Step 6: Add the ornament top back on and paint white or cream frosting using acrylic paint. Once dry add sprinkles with acrylic paint or paint markers.

Step 7: Add a cute face using paint markers or acrylic paint.

Step 8: Glue the ornament to a cupcake liner. I just glue the bottom but you could also add a little glue on the sides if needed.

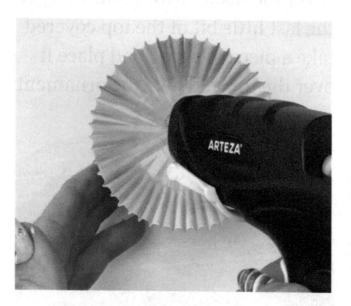

Jenga Snowmen Ornaments

SUPPLIES:

- Wooden blocks
- A scarf or scrap fabric
- Small googly eyes
- Small foam paintbrush
- Small detail brush
- Hot glue gun
- White paint
- Orange paint
- Black paint
- Twine
- Scissors

Step 1: Using the small foam brush, paint the blocks white. Let dry. Paint two coats if needed, drying in between coats.

Step 2: While they are drying, cut 8 small pieces of the scarf to the size you would like. (About the length of 2 blocks and the width of the skinner side of a block.)

Step 3: Glue the eyes at the top of the block.

Step 4: Using the detail brush, paint a small orange triangle for the nose and small black dots for the mouth. At the bottom, paint 3 dots for the buttons. Let dry.

Step 5: After the blocks have dried, add a dot of glue to the middle of the back of the ornament and secure the scarf. Wrap around and glue in the front. Fold the scarf and secure it with glue.

Step 6: Cut pieces of twine about 2 inches.
Step 7: Make a loop and glue it to the top of the back of ornament.

Popsicle Stick Nutcrackers

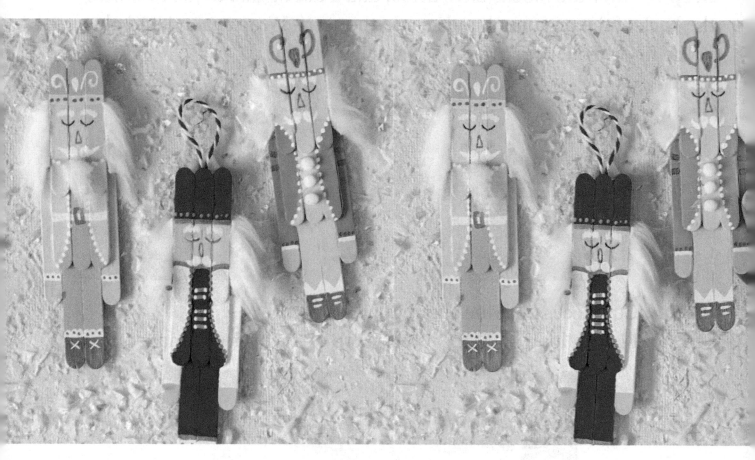

SUPPLIES:

- 8 small craft sticks
- 2 regular craft sticks
- Watercolor paint
- Small paint brushes
- White fax fur
- Twine, ribbon or string for hanging
- Hot glue gun
- Paint pens

Step 1: Begin by gluing the popsicle sticks together as shown in the diagram below.

1. Place the two longest sticks side by side.
2. Add hot glue to one small craft stick, then place it on top of the two long sticks, centered and with the top edges lined up.
3. Add hot glue on either side of the small stick and press two more small sticks down, lining up the ends.
4. Glue two small sticks underneath, so they're even with the long sticks, but attached to the three small sticks in front.
5. Place glue along the top edge, then attach three more sticks, lining the bottom edges up so they're about 1/3 overlapping the other sticks.

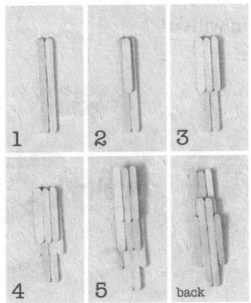

Step 2: Once all of the sticks are glued together, it's time to add some color and personality. Paint the top of the nutcracker to look like his hat, then leave his face area raw wood. Paint the rest of the nutcracker light green, then when that is dry, add dark green sleeves and a curved area to look like a jacket.

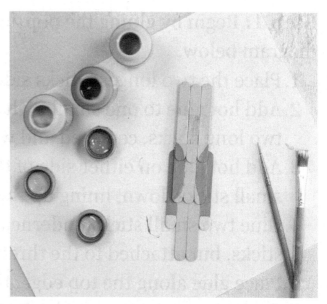

Step 3: Using paint pens, add in all the cute details. Add eyes, a nose and a bushy mustache. Then fill in details like sleeve cuffs, hat bands, shoelaces, etc. Have fun with it!

Step 4: Cut tiny little strips of faux fur and hot glue them to the sides of the face area to give the nutcracker some hair.

TIP: If you've never crafted with faux fur before, try cutting it from the back side. Slide the tip of your scissors just under the backing fabric so you aren't actually cutting the fur, just the backing.

Step 5: Use hot glue to attach a twine loop onto the back of nutcracker if you plan to use it as an ornament. If not, you can skip this step.

Candy Cane Paintings

SUPPLIES:
- Watercolor paper
- Red paint
- White paint
- Green paint
- Pencil
- Eraser
- Small paint brushes

Step 1: Sketch the motif in pencil to make it easier to paint later.

Step 2: Mix a nice shade of red on your color palette and start coloring the red areas step by step. Start with a lot of water and little color.

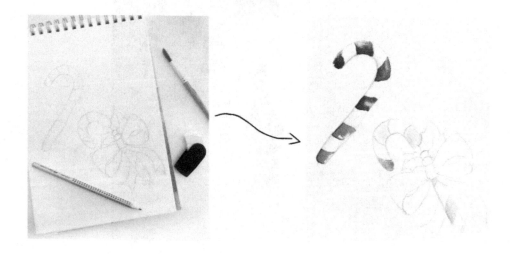

Step 3: Add more color layer by layer – this will create light and shadow at the edges.

Step 4: Let the red areas dry a little and while you wait, mix a nice color for your bow. Again, start with a lot of water and a little color.

Step 5: Using a darker tone or more paint than water, you can now carefully color all the areas that are in shadow. This creates a three-dimensional effect and makes the motif appear more realistic.

Step 6: Let your bow dry a little so that the colors don't mix and start with your leaves. Again, layer by layer and from light to dark.

Step 7: Using more and more color and darker tones, you can now rework the shadows and structure of the leaves. After a short drying time, you can paint the berries in a beautiful red.

Step 8: Watercolor paints can be dissolved with water. So you can now use your wet brush to dissolve the paint in a circular motion in the areas that should be lighter and dab it off with a tissue. This will give you the lighter areas of your motif.

Reindeer Clothpins

SUPPLIES:

- Glue gun
- Glue sticks
- Paintbrush
- Scissors
- 4 Clothespins, Wooden Spring Style
- Dark brown paint
- 4 Googly Eyes
- Mini Pom Poms - red
- Mini holly leaves and berries
- Natural jute twine
- Skinny ribbon

Step 1: First, assemble all of your supplies. Remove the metal springs from your standard wooden clothespins. Each reindeer requires two full clothespins, and you'll need to line them up on your work area to make a V shape.

Step 2: Next, glue the clothespin pieces together using your hot glue gun.

Step 3: The next step is to paint the body of the reindeer with brown acrylic paint. You can use any shade of brown you like best. Acrylic paint dries relatively quickly, which is nice if you find that the clothespins need a second coat.

Step 4: After your clothespins are fully dried, the next steps are to use small drops of hot glue to attach the googly eyes and the red pom pom nose.

Step 5: Now it's time to add a little bit of personality to your clothespin reindeer pair. Tie the skinny plaid ribbon into a bow and glue it to one reindeer's neck. Attach the mini holly leaf and red berries to the side of the clothespin on the second reindeer.

Step 6: Once your little reindeer is completely assembled, you're ready to glue on the twine. Cut 12" of natural twine and tie in a circle. Then glue the loop to the back of the reindeer, making sure each one is large enough to easily fit on a Christmas tree branch.

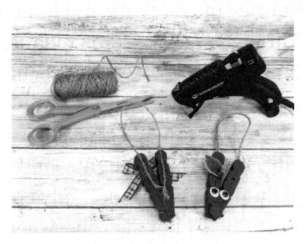

Step 7: Now your adorable reindeer ornaments are ready to go on the Christmas tree!

Thank you

Creative DIY Watercolor Christmas: Easy and Enjoyable Projects Coloring Your Own Holidays has been a delightful journey of creativity and holiday cheer. Through step-by-step guidance and inspiring images, you've brought the magic of Christmas to life on canvas.

As you've painted scenes of snow-covered villages, twinkling lights, and festive gatherings, you've not only created beautiful works of art but also cherished memories. This book has been a wonderful companion, encouraging you to express your unique vision of Christmas and embrace the joy of painting. Whether you're a seasoned artist or a beginner just starting out, **Creative DIY Watercolor Christmas** has provided a fulfilling and rewarding experience. So, grab your brushes, choose your colors, and continue to let your imagination run wild as you create your own personal Christmas wonderland.

Made in United States
Orlando, FL
03 December 2024

54885421R00043